Working with Visually Disabled People: bridging theory and practice

Sally French, Maureen Gillman & John Swain

VENTURE PRESS

Acknowledgements

We are grateful to the many people who helped us to make this book a reality. We would like to thank all the people we interviewed for the openness with which they talked about their lives and shared their thoughts and ideas. Their stories and experiences contributed in a very major way to this book. The people we interviewed are: Ayesha Vernon, Stephanie Argyraki, Sue and Paul Nicholls, Olwen Mitchelson, Joan Wilson, and Alan Dudley.

Our thanks are also extended to Laura Middleton for her helpful comments on an earlier draft and her support throughout

Contents

Published by
VENTURE PRESS
16 Kent Street
Birmingham
B5 6RD

British Library Cataloguing-in-Publication Data
A catalogue record for this book is available from the British Library

ISBN 1-86178-014-1 (paperback)

Design, layout and production by
Hucksters Advertising & Publishing Consultants,
Riseden, Tidebrook, Wadhurst, East Sussex TN5 6PA

Cover design by:
Western Arts
194 Goswell Road
London
EC1V 7DT

Printed in Great Britain

Introduction

We have written this guide about visual disability from a civil rights perspective. Our aim has been to work within the theoretical and practical perspectives of visually disabled people themselves - to allow their voice to be heard. Our discussions are under-pinned by the social model of disability, where disability is viewed as stemming from social and physical barriers within the environment rather than from the individual's impairment. All of our discussions have been informed by the growing voice of the Disabled People's Movement. Two of the authors, Maureen Gillman and Sally French, are themselves visually disabled.

The guide is in three sections. The first section *In Theory* discusses theoretical issues of relevance to a thorough understanding of visual disability. This section discusses the nature of theory; positive and negative language, symbols and imagery, the diversity of visually disabled people, their collective experiences with other disabled people, and the types of support mechanisms provided through history including recent legislation and the campaign for civil rights.

Section two of the guide consists of six short case studies of visually disabled people written from open-ended interviews.

Section three *In Practice* links the theoretical discussion and the case studies to professional practice. The level and type of support that Social Service departments and other agencies offer visually disabled people is discussed and guidelines are given for reflective, anti-discriminatory and anti-oppressive practice.

In theory

WHAT'S IN A THEORY?

There are numerous different theories of visual disability. At its broadest it can be argued that there are as many theories as there are human beings where 'theory' is an individual's understanding of visual disability. Even within this statement, however, there are more collective understandings, as evidenced by the very use of the term 'visual disability'. Furthermore, a distinction can be made between theories arising directly from experience of visual disability, and those emanating from, for instance, professionals who work with visually disabled people. Another complicating factor is the differentiation between theory and action. What people believe and understand stands in complex relation to what they actually do. A final complication is the purpose of theories. To recognise this dimension of theory is to acknowledge that all theories have political import. There is no such thing as neutral theory. Every theory of visual disability speaks to the establishment of shared 'social understanding', justifies particular practices and policies, and is integral to power relations between people.

THEORY FROM EXPERIENCE OF DISABILITY

The crucial development in theories of visual disability over at least the past twenty years has been the establishment of the social model of disability.

There are a number of key features to this:

1. The social model of disability recognises the social origins of disability in a society geared by and for non-disabled people. The first clear and principled statement of the social model is generally thought to be the statement by *The Union of the*

Physically Impaired Against Segregation (UPIAS) and took the form, centrally, of two definitions:

Impairment. *Lacking part or all of a limb, or having a defective limb, organ or mechanism of the body,* and

Disability. *The disadvantage or restriction of activity caused by a contemporary social organisation which takes no or little account of people who have physical impairments and thus excludes them from participation in the mainstream of social activities. Physical disability is therefore a particular form of social oppression.*

(UPIAS 1976:14)

In the social model the disadvantages or restrictions, often referred to as barriers, permeate every aspect of the physical and social environment: attitudes, institutions, language and culture, organisation and delivery of support services, and the power relationships and structures of which society is constituted (Swain et al 1993). The model has gained widespread acceptance though, as Oliver (1996) points out, this is in theory only and whether it has had much impact on professional practice is another question entirely.

2. The social model has increasingly been applied to all disabled people irrespective of specific impairments.
   As Oliver states:

   All disabled people experience disability as social restriction, whether those restrictions occur as a consequence of inaccessible built environments... the lack of reading material in Braille or hostile public attitudes to people with non-visible disabilities.

   (1990: xiv)

Thus the social model sites visual disability as social restriction which isolates and precludes visually disabled people from full participation in society, rather than being a result of conditions of the eye. In doing so, it aligns visually disabled people with all disabled people whose oppression can be understood in the same general terms.

3. This model or theory of visual disability has arisen from the experiences of disabled people themselves. It is borne out of their collective experience challenging *'the way they have been defined and controlled by the experts who manipulate disability policy'* (Davis 1993:289).
It is no coincidence that the Disabled People's Movement and the social model of disability have developed together. The social model emanates from the pooled experience and discussion of oppression. As Rachel Hurst of *Disabled People's International* states:

> *When you come together with other disabled people, you have the time and the opportunity to discuss what the situation really is – what oppression is, who is oppressing you; where oppression comes from, what discrimination is and where it comes from.*
>
> **(Coleridge 1993:54)**

The social model stands in direct opposition to the dominant individual model of visual disability, which encompasses tragedy and medical models. As well as being grounded in the collective experience of disabled people, the social model of disability promotes personal and political empowerment. It engenders self-confidence and pride, rather than the guilt and shame associated with the tragedy model. The political implications of the social model, often explicitly stated, are to promote the collective struggle by disabled people for social change. One measure for the effectiveness of the model has been the proliferation of the Disabled People's Movement and the burgeoning of not only many small organisations throughout the world but also national organisations, for example the *British Council of Disabled People*, and international organisations, for example *Disabled People's International*, all of which are organised and controlled by disabled people and exist for disabled people.

As a collective, dynamic theory, the social model is undergoing continued development. As is perhaps inevitable within social movements engaged in active debate, the Disabled People's Movement has continued to address challenges to both the organisation of the movement and its theoretical foundations. Criticisms have been voiced by disabled people on a number of grounds, though it is crucial to recognise that all such critics accept the basic principles of the social model and are arguing for a development, extension or renewal of the model.

The main critique addresses a need to recognise, respect, respond to and indeed celebrate difference (Morris 1991) while maintaining solidarity against the commonality of oppression. There are two main lines of debate. The first centres on the experience of different forms of oppression and the establishment of different group identities. Gender, race and sexual preference are significant to disabled people's experiences of oppression. Shakespeare states,

> *'I still think it is dangerous to overlook multiple identities, and to assume that disability is the sole and significant identity.'*
>
> *(1996:110)*

Shakespeare et al (1996) argue that the Disabled People's Movement needs to adapt and change to be fully representative, but they also suggest that other movements and communities, particularly the women's movement and the gay and lesbian movement, also need to adapt and recognise their disabled members.

The second form of critique argues that the Disabled People's Movement and the social model of disability should take a wider approach to cover other aspects of disabled people's lives including relationships, sexuality and experiences directly related to impairment such as pain. Crow, for instance, states:

> *This model would operate on two levels: a more complete understanding of disability and impairment as social concepts, and a recognition of an individual's experiences of their body over time and in variable circumstances.*
>
> *(1996:218)*

The crucial point to be made about these debates, in the context of the present discussion, is that they reflect the voices of disabled people themselves, attempting to generate a new discourse about themselves and taking control of the development of theory.

PERSONAL ACTION THEORIES

The first line of development in understanding and exploring 'what is a theory?' by professionals working with visually disabled people is, then, generated by disabled people themselves. The second, to which we now turn, addresses the nature of professional development and incorporates the re-assessment of the relationship between theory and practice.

The traditional model of professional development has separated theory from practice and perpetuated their separation. In more recent years, however, this has been broken down through the notion of 'reflective practice' which has been encompassed within and propagated through widespread developments in professional training. Schön (1988) distinguishes in some detail between two models of professional development.

Model 1, sometimes called the traditional model, involves the following action strategies for the professional providing social support: design and manage the environment so that the professional is in control of the factors which he or she sees as relevant; own and control the task; unilaterally protect self by, for instance, withholding critical information; and unilaterally protect others, particularly the client, from being hurt. Schön associated this model with what he calls 'single loop' learning,

'Learning about strategies or tactics for achieving one's own objectives.'

(1988:256).

Model 2, or the reflective practice model, is characterised by quite different action strategies: design situations in which all participants, particularly the professional and client working in partnership, participate in defining and controlling relevant factors; the task is jointly controlled; protection of self is a joint enterprise, orientated towards growth and bilateral protection of others.

The challenge to professionals who work with visually disabled people is to construct services and practices which respond to the viewpoint of visually disabled people. What are the implications of a social model for professional practice? Three key principles are evident:

- The social model demands a shift of power to disabled people.
- The focus for intervention is the dismantling of disabling barriers and the creation of enabling environments.
- Social support to visually disabled people is orientated to their rights to full participative citizenship (rights not 'special needs').

DIVERSITY AND THEORY

We will concentrate next on the diversity of visual impairment and visual disability and the variability in the lives and experiences of visually disabled people. This is of central importance to social workers and other professionals who work with visually disabled clients as unique individuals. We will also argue that there is commonality within this diversity and that the central feature of this commonality is oppression. Oppression is not only a shared experience of visually disabled people but of all disabled people throughout the world. This discussion will bring us back to the social model of disability.

INDIVIDUAL DIFFERENCES

The experience of visual disability differs greatly from one person to another so it is unwise to treat visually disabled people in the same way. A minority of people are born visually impaired and, therefore, do not know life in any other way, while the majority acquire visual impairment, usually in later life (Bruce et al 1991). Visual impairment can occur suddenly, for example as the result of an accident, or very gradually over a number of years. People who acquire a visual impairment may feel an acute sense of loss in certain areas of their lives and according to their lifestyles. They may, for example, greatly miss being able to read print or to do their shopping unaided. People who are visually impaired from birth or early childhood are unlikely to feel a sense of loss although they may be fully aware of the limitations society imposes upon them.

It is not easy to understand what visually disabled people can see because this will depend on their particular eye condition. Seeing is also an intellectual activity where images which reach the retina are interpreted by the brain. Visually disabled people may thus learn to 'see' better as time goes by. Some visually disabled people can see small print but are unable to recognise a friend or see a street name or house number. Some people can see quite well in daylight but hardly at all at night, while for others this is reversed. Visually disabled people may have a restricted field of vision, for example tunnel vision or peripheral vision, and may or may not be able to appreciate colour. The requirements of visually disabled people are, therefore, very diverse.

Visually disabled people also have different degrees of vision from 'useful' vision to total blindness. Only four per cent of visually disabled people have no sight at all. People with very limited vision tend to operate more as sighted than as blind people and people with light perception are in a markedly different position from those who are totally blind. They are able, for example, to orientate themselves by the light from a window.

Some visually disabled people know they will retain the sight they have while others must face the prospect of total blindness or the slow deterioration of their vision. For some people the amount that they see changes from day to day making it even more difficult for other people to understand their situation. Visual impairment can also be associated with unpleasant symptoms like pain, or other impairments such as arthritis and diabetes. More than fifty per cent of visually disabled children have additional impairments such as deafness and learning difficulties (Walker et al 1992). Most visually disabled people are not ill and it is important not to associate visual disability with illness.

It is important to realise that being visually disabled is just one attribute of the individual which interacts with all other attributes. An outgoing visually disabled person may, for example, have different ways of coping than someone who is quiet and reserved. Visually disabled people, like other disabled people, are often stereotyped and thought of as a group. Although visual disability can be a very central experience, visually disabled people are as unique as all other people.

GROUP DIFFERENCES

Visually disabled people are not confined to any particular group within society but are present regardless of gender, ethnicity, social class, sexual orientation and age. The experience of visual disability may, however, be different according to these broad divisions. Visually disabled women may, for example, find themselves under particular pressures not to have children and may find it more difficult to obtain paid employment than visually disabled men because of sexist attitudes (Morris 1991). Visually disabled men may, on the other hand, find it more difficult to ask for help because of the stereotyped 'macho' role of competence and power. They may also feel the consequences of unemployment more acutely than disabled women.

Ethnicity may also interact with visual disability giving rise to particularly oppressive experiences. It is well known that, because of racist attitudes, people from ethnic minorities are treated less well as patients and clients in the health and social services and find it more difficult to obtain paid employment (Begum et al 1994). These problems are exacerbated for visually disabled people from ethnic minority groups who may be coping with disablist attitudes too and may not identify either with their own non-disabled community or with disabled people from the white ethnic majority (Stuart 1993). This has led to the formation of various organisations of people from ethnic minority groups such as *The Association of Blind Asians*.

Visually disabled women from ethnic minority groups are in a particularly difficult situation as they may be coping with sexist, racist and disablist attitudes and practices. It is important, however, not to view these oppressions as adding one to the other; Morris (1991), Stuart (1993) and Begum (1994) point out that disabled women and disabled people from minority ethnic groups experience a unique form of oppression which is more than the sum of the parts.

Some visually disabled people are lesbian and gay and may have particular difficulties in establishing satisfying personal and sexual relationships. Visual disability makes social interaction difficult. This is not only because of the difficulty of recognising people and reading non-verbal cues, but also because of attitudes towards visual disability, difficulties in getting to social venues, unemployment and mobility problems, for example being unable to circulate at a social gathering (Shakespeare et al 1996). Visually disabled people who are lesbian or gay may have particular difficulties as the processes involved in meeting suitable partners are often more discreet. This difficulty has prompted the formation of various organisations such as *GEMNA* (for disabled lesbians) and *VIGG* (a support group of visually disabled gay people).

The majority of visually disabled people are over the age of 65 and may find themselves contending with ageism as well as disablism. They may be told, for example, that they can expect nothing more 'at their age' or that they must accept the inevitable consequences of degenerative disease. This is clearly illustrated in two of the case studies in the next section of the guide. The resources made available for older visually disabled people tend to be less than that for younger people even though coping with a visual disability may be more difficult because, for example, of reduced hearing or mobility.

Social class may also have an influence on how visual disability is experienced. Visual impairment is present among people of all social classes but, like most impairments, it is more prevalent among people of low socio-economic class. This reflects the higher incidence of prematurity, birth trauma, infectious diseases, accidents and poverty and illustrates that impairment, as well as disability is, at least in part, socially constructed.

As we have already explained, visual disability does not arise directly from visual impairment but is an interaction between visual impairment and various social and environmental barriers within society. The higher the social position a visually disabled person, or a visually disabled child's family, has within society the more able he or she is to remove these barriers. A person who is employed and receiving a high salary, for example, will be able to afford taxis to get about, will be able to purchase visual aids and equipment and may pay for some assistance, for example to do the gardening or decorate the house. Visually disabled people in this position tend to be in the minority, however, because only approximately 25% of visually disabled people of working age are in paid employment and the majority of visually disabled people are over retirement age (Bruce et al 1991).

The advantage of being from a higher social class does not only concern financial resources. The experience of a more privileged up-bringing and lifestyle including, for example, a good education and socialisation within a profession, tends to make people feel more confident about themselves and better equipped to demand their rights. They are less likely to be intimidated by professionals and are more likely to understand the workings of, for example, the Social Services department.

DIVERSITY AND QUESTIONS OF THEORY

We have so far looked at specific and broad differences among visually disabled people. Despite this diversity visually disabled people throughout the world share many common experiences of oppression and discrimination which are shared too with those with other impairments such as deafness, learning difficulties and language impairments. These oppressive experiences include discrimination in terms of education, leisure and employment, hostile attitudes, institutionalisation, poverty and lack of access to transport. The social model of disability and the Disabled People's Movement has focused on these collective experiences and have drawn disabled people, with different impairments, together throughout the world. This collective struggle has brought about many changes in Britain and throughout the world including the passing, in many countries, of anti-discrimination legislation. A limited form of anti-discrimination legislation was brought into force in Britain in 1995.

The coming together of disabled people in a collective struggle has also been important in dispelling the common belief, often voiced by government, that disabled people differ so greatly in terms of impairment that they do not form a coherent social group. It has also challenged the individual model of disability where disability is viewed as resulting from individual impairment which can be 'overcome' or reduced by helping disabled people to become more 'normal'.

IMAGES, SYMBOLS AND WORDS

A broad definition of theory encompasses what might be called 'implicit theory' as well as formal statements. Implicit theories include understandings of visual disability conveyed in the daily bombardment of images through the media, visual arts, drama, language and so on, that is cultural conceptions of visual disability within western society. For many people implicit theory is their only contact with visual disability. As Dodds states,

> *'All that most people have to go on are images of blindness perpetuated by the media, visual arts, literature and drama.'*
>
> *(1993:6)*

The overall negative view of disabled people as a threat to the well-being of the non-disabled community is part of the context in which sighted people not only respond to visually disabled people, but also to becoming visually impaired and having a visually impaired child. Implicit theory is also, however, the context in which disabled people collectively promote alternative understandings of visual disability. The Disabled People's Movement has challenged implicit theory by making it explicit and producing its own images to promote the social model of disability.

DISABLING IMAGES

The oppressive and disabling nature of cultural images of disability have increasingly been subjected to analysis by disabled people (Hevey 1992). Barnes (1993), from his research of media images, has documented examples of eleven cultural stereotypes which perpetuate the linkage between impairment and 'all that is socially unacceptable'. Three seem particularly pertinent to the theories implicit in depictions of visually disabled people.

First, the most frequently cited example of the commonly recurring image of visually disabled people as 'sinister and evil' has been Blind Pew in R.L. Stevenson's *Treasure Island* (Rieser 1995). More recent examples are to be found in a *Fighting Fantasy Gamebook* entitled *Out of the Pit* (Jackson and Livingstone 1995). The eyes are the most frequently mentioned feature of this book of descriptions of fantasy monsters. Some, such as the Cyclops and Medusa, have quite well known historical antecedents, and many descriptions mention the eyes signifying an evil, controlling influence, for example by glowing red.

A second commonly recurring image of visually disabled people is as objects of ridicule. This usually involves typical slap-stick humour with the visually disabled person bumping into objects, breaking things, falling into holes, not recognising people and generally causing havoc. The cartoon character *Mr. Magoo* is an obvious example. A whole BBC television series called Clarence, with the central character being played by Ronnie Barker, was founded on such comedy, and a similar character regularly appeared in the popular series *The Last of the Summer Wine*.

A third recurring image is that of visually disabled people as pitiable and pathetic. An example in the visual arts is Sir John Everett Milais's painting of *The Blind Girl*. The central figure wears a notice around her neck that reads 'Pity the blind'. As Dodds states:

'The over-riding emotion is of that of an infinite sadness for someone who can never see what we as viewers can; the rainbow, the birds, the stream, and most poignant of all, her own beauty.' (1993:8)

The implicit theory of visual disability conveyed within these cultural images has a number of key elements:

- It is almost entirely negative and built around stereotypes which dehumanise and degrade.
- It focuses on the individual.
- Impairment is equated with disability.
- It denies the experiences of disabled people themselves and the discrimination and oppression they face in a disabling society.

The theory of disability as conveyed by such images is implicit, that is it has a prime purpose other than portraying the meaning of visual disability. This is, perhaps, most obvious in advertising by charities. Research at the King's Fund Centre (Scott-Parker 1986) showed that the prime purpose of images of disabled people in advertisements was fund raising. The study also showed that the charities had no research evidence that pitiable and pathetic images motivate non-disabled people to donate more money. Images in the creative arts also have their own purposes. Again, it is not the intent to convey an explicitly espoused theory of visual disability, but rather to enhance the impact of the painting, play, story and so on. Blind Pew, for instance, was not depicted as a blind character to convey specifically an understanding of blindness, but rather to use (and hence propagate) stereotypes of blind people in creating a threatening figure within the story line. It is also worth noting that these implicit theories are constructed mainly by non-disabled, sighted people.

Disabling words

The creation of negative images of visual disability and the perpetuation of stereotypes are also conveyed in everyday speech (French 1989). Words, phrases, and discourse can, again, be considered as reflecting implicit theories of visual disability. The debates around the use of language are not simply technical issues over the use of terminology, or issues of 'political correctness' of whether one word or phrase should be used in preference to another word or phrase. They are political debates which are, in effect, part of the struggle to establish and legitimate one way of thinking over another. Oliver cites the work of the French philosopher Foucault to convey the importance of this political debate:

> *The way we talk about the world and the way we experience it are inextricable linked - the names we give to things shapes our experience of them and our experience of things in the world influences the names we give to them.*
>
> *(1996:72)*

In this light there is little wonder that the use of language and the changing of discourse has been so crucial to the Disabled People's Movement in establishing a social model of disability.

Disablist language varies in meaning and use, and is expressed through a variety of media, including literature, television, cinema, drama, legislation and political discourse, and everyday language. The use of disabling terms varies, too, from the implicit images within commonly used phrases, to the directly abusive use of devaluing terms. What is shared in all disabling language is the promotion of negative images which 'perpetuate discriminatory attitudes and practices among the general public' (Barnes 1993:41) and, it can be added, among those providing social support for visually disabled people.

An insidious and difficult to control form of disablist language is that within everyday speech. Phrases such as 'the blind leading the blind', 'blind drunk', 'blind stupidity' and 'she's being short-sighted' construct images which are derogatory and also factually false. Visually disabled people, for instance, generally know the best ways of leading and directing other visually disabled people.

More direct references to visually disabled people and visual disability can be disablist in a number of ways:

- Language may be abusive in the straightforward way of being insulting, for example 'four-eyes'.
- Disability may be equated with impairment, effectively denying the institutional discrimination and oppression experienced by disabled people, for example 'he's an albino'.
- Disability and impairment terms may be used as nouns to refer to people rather than as adjectives. For example, many charities, including the *Royal National Institute for The Blind* use the disability term to refer to people and thus dehumanise and objectify. As French states '*It is as if the disability is the most important, if not the only attribute, the individual possesses.*' (1989:29)
- Adjectives may be used to describe visually disabled people which promotes an individual, tragic view of visual disability, for example 'suffering'.

In their campaign to eliminate the use of disabling language, the *British Council of Disabled People* have adopted strategies such as publishing a *Disability Etiquette* which includes, for instance, that the word disabled is not used as a noun.

Somewhat more complex and ephemeral is the discourse in which social support is constructed. Yet the use of disablist language is crucial to the justification, organisation and practice of social support for visually disabled people. A debate which disabled people have brought to centre stage is encapsulated by the phrase **'Rights not Special Needs'**. The discourse of needs focuses on the individual and the provision of social support which addresses, in theory, the individual's lack of capabilities to function within his or her particular community and society generally. The discourse of rights focuses on disabled people as a distinctive group within our society, who are denied their rights through institutional discrimination.

LIBERATING IMAGES

Disability Arts is a relatively recent, though well established, part of the Disabled People's Movement. A wide diversity of activities are encompassed within disability arts. There are a growing number of examples of the work of individual artists expressing their experiences and communicating their thoughts and feelings, as disabled people, in poems, paintings and so on. A central feature of Disability Arts, however, is collective experience. Disabled people are increasingly coming together to help each other express themselves in music, drama, forms of visual arts and comedy. Through Disability Arts many visually disabled people have regular opportunities to share ideas and information with each other and other disabled people.

In terms of theory of visual disability, Disability Arts is a political as well as an artistic forum and, as such, seems to have four major functions:

1 Disability Arts involve making the implicit theories of visual disability explicit, exposing the derogatory nature of negative images and stereotypes of disabled people.

2 Disability Arts has also, often through humour, lampooned

and challenged disabling attitudes and forms of discrimination and oppression.

3   Through their writing, visual and performing arts, disabled people are also promoting very different images of disability which celebrate differences between people and promote the value of all people. Disability Arts, then, has furthered the exploration of a social model of disability.

4   The active participation of disabled people in Disability Arts in itself combats images of passivity and dependence. The empowering role of Disability Arts is described by Morrison and Finkelstein:

"The arts can have a liberating effect on people, encouraging them to change from being passive and dependent to being creative and active... meeting together at a disability arts event can also provide rare opportunities for disabled people to exchange ideas".

(1993:127)

WELFARE AND SUPPORT

The history of welfare provision for disabled people, including visually disabled people, is difficult to trace. Although there is a huge medical history and many official documents celebrating 'good works' there has been little interest in the experience of disability which, until recent times, remained virtually undocumented. We shall briefly trace the history of welfare provision for disabled people from charitable and state provision, to a consideration of the role disabled people have played in securing their own citizenship and civil rights.

CAP IN HAND

The Poor Law of 1601 marked the first official recognition of the need for state intervention in the lives of disabled people. Until then, if support from their families was lacking, disabled people were entirely dependent on haphazard gifts of charity for their subsistence and many were forced to beg.

With the coming of the Industrial Revolution disabled people found it even more difficult to find employment and to support themselves. Work was heavier, speed was more important and work was done away from home. The increased numbers of disabled people (and others) without work put the system of parish relief under stain and in 1834 the Poor Law Amendment Act was passed which centralised services. The policy under this Act was one of referral to workhouses for those who were unable to work or support themselves. Institutional provision thus increased greatly at this time.

At the end of the 19th century there was an upsurge of Christian morality and humanitarianism and people with specific impairments, such as visual impairment, were singled out for special attention by rich philanthropists who often worked with religious establishments to provide the funds for segregated homes and schools. A large number of charitable organisations were established at this time, for example *The Royal National Institute for the Blind*.

In the early years of the welfare state many other charities and institutions were established, for example *St Dunstan's for Men and Women Blinded in War Service* and the *Leonard Cheshire Foundation*. This increase led to a proliferation of professionals such as teachers, physiotherapists, and clinical psychologists. The dominance of these professionals led to an increasing tendency to individualise and medicalise the lives of disabled people. Doctors, for example, became involved in decisions which had little to do with medicine such as educational provision and the suitability of employment and housing.

Services for disabled people, including visually disabled people, have their origins, therefore, in the surplus time and money of the wealthy and the post-war development of the health and welfare professions (Morris 1991). These organisations and professional bodies are locked in a partnership with the state and operate within an individual model of disability which assumes that disabled people cannot take charge of their own lives. This way of thinking and the resulting policies and services which are provided have led disabled people to become unnecessarily dependent.

LEGISLATING FOR NEEDS

The depression of the 1930s and the Second World War gave the impetus for much new legislation some of which had an impact on disabled people. This legislation included the 1944 Employment Act which introduced the quota system, obliging employers with twenty or more workers to discriminate in favour of disabled people, the 1944 Education Act which obliged local authorities to provide special schooling for children thought to need it, the National Health Service Act (1948) designed to meet the medical needs of ill and disabled people, as well as providing aids and equipment, and the National Assistance Act (1948) designed to supply residential accommodation and other services for disabled people and to assist with their financial needs.

A major recent piece of legislation is the 1990 National Health Service and Community Care Act. This Act affirms the value of a non-institutionalised and non-segregated lifestyle and the ideal that disabled people should make their own decisions and achieve their full potential. It acknowledges that services should be sensitive, flexible and tailored to the needs of the individual. The Act formulates a move away from service-led towards needs-led provision, where the needs of individuals determine what kind of services they receive.

The professionals who assess the needs of disabled people are no longer the providers of the service which, in theory at least, may increase choice. Assessment is still the gateway to services, however, and there is no automatic provision, but if a need is identified the local authority is legally obliged to provide it. A new breed of professionals called 'care managers' draw up a 'care plan' based on an assessment for each disabled person entitled to it. The care plan is, in theory, intended to ensure that the needs of individual disabled people are met. An important recent development in community care is direct payment to disabled people whereby they can purchase their own care as they see fit (Zarb 1995). This Act does not, however, appear to have had a great deal of impact on the lives of visually disabled people. Lovelock et al (1995) confirm from their research that low priority is given to visually disabled people and that provision is generally of a poor quality and has not changed significantly in the last few years. Some of the case studies in section two of this guide confirm this view.

Many disabled people believe that this legislation, like that of the past, is both paternalistic and dependency creating (Davis 1994). Disabled people still have to go through a professional to attempt to acquire what other people may take for granted. Disabled people argue that money would be better spent in removing the social and physical barriers within society which prevent their full participation in everyday life. If the environment were adapted disabled people would be in a far better position to earn their own living which many people have found possible when they gain direct access to funding (Oliver and Zarb 1992).

In 1995 the Disability Discrimination Act was passed. This is, unfortunately, a very weak piece of legislation with no enforcement body such as a commission. Important areas of life, such as education and transport, have virtually been excluded. The government's main objection to fully comprehensive anti-discrimination legislation has been the cost of implementation and the view that the concerns of disabled people, by virtue of their different impairments, are totally unrelated making comprehensive legislation too complicated (Zarb 1995). The Act does to a limited extent, however, cover employment and the supply of goods and services. It is, for example, unlawful to refuse a visually disabled person with a guide dog in a restaurant or to treat disabled people less favourably in terms of their promotion at work.

MOVING FOR RIGHTS

Disabled people constitute, potentially, a powerful political force; yet because of the widespread discrimination against them, in terms of education, employment, transport and so on, they have been rendered relatively powerless. This situation is, however, beginning to change. As facilities have gradually improved over the past twenty years, disabled people have come together to campaign for change and a strong Disabled People's Movement has emerged (Campbell and Oliver 1996). Many visually disabled people are active members of this movement.

The Disabled People's Movement consists of organisations **of** disabled people, that is organisations which are controlled by disabled people themselves, although many welcome non-disabled allies. This is in contrast to organisation **for** disabled people such as *The Royal National Institute for the Blind*. An early organisation of disabled people in Britain was the *The National League of the Blind* which was founded in 1899. Over the next sixty years, many other organisations of disabled people developed. They usually focused on specific impairments or single issues, such as lack of state provision. During the 1960s and 1970s, organisations **of** disabled people which crossed impairment boundaries began to develop; the issue which drew them together was poverty.

Perhaps the most significant turning point in the Disabled People's Movement was the formation in 1974 of *The Union of the Physically Impaired Against Segregation* (UPIAS). Davis (1993) explains how UPIAS fought to change the definition of disability from one of individual tragedy to one of social oppression. This paved the way for the development of the social model of disability.

In 1981 *The British Council of Organisation of Disabled People* (BCODP), an umbrella group of disabled people, was formed. This organisation, now called *The British Council of Disabled People*, continues to expand and now represents some 112 organisations and over 200,000 disabled people. One of these organisations in Britain is *The National Federation of the Blind*. *The British Council of Disabled People* is recognised as the representative voice of disabled people in Britain.

1981 also saw the birth of *Disabled People's International* (DPI). This umbrella organisation represents over 70 national assembles of disabled people throughout the world and is recognised by the United Nations as the representative voice of disabled people internationally.

Oliver (1995) points to growing evidence that a new kind of welfare state is emerging which will be based on rights, entitlements and consumer control.

Case studies

This section of the guide consists of six short case studies of visually disabled people. They have been written using open-ended interviews. They do not comprise a representative sample but, by choosing people of different ages, cultural backgrounds, lifestyles and experiences, we have tried to illustrate the diversity of visually disabled people. These case studies will help practitioners to develop a broad view of visual disability, and the lives and experiences of visually disabled people, which we believe is essential for successful practice. Each case study is in three parts consisting of a brief biographical introduction, the personal experience of being visually disabled, and the strategies used for overcoming or minimising visual disability. We hope that they will bring alive theoretical and practical issues in professional practice and allow visually disabled people to speak for themselves.

AYESHA VERNON

Ayesha was born in 1965 in a rural village in India where she lived with her grandparents. Ayesha's family were poor owning just a small plot of land for their subsistence. At the age of four Ayesha developed meningitis. When she recovered from the illness she was left visually impaired seeing nothing but light and vague shapes. She was the only visually disabled person in her village.

There was no provision for visually disabled children in the village where Ayesha lived and, despite a love of learning, she was not accepted at the local school. Instead she stayed at home and helped the neighbours with their household and child care tasks. Ayesha believes that her neighbours played a crucial role in her early development:

My grandmother used to portray me as useless... but the neighbours, by letting me help them with washing and perhaps having a go at making a chapatti, made me feel that what my grandmother said wasn't true and that I

*could do something if someone gave me the chance. That
was very important in my development.*

At the age of fourteen Ayesha came to England where her
father was working and for the first time received a formal
education. She had home tuition in braille and English for
six months and then went to a residential school for
visually disabled children:

*I could only speak very basic English. Communication
was very difficult, I was the only Asian girl there. I had
kids laughing at my English and I had difficulty making
them understand what I wanted. Culturally it was very
different. I ate Asian food. I wore Asian clothes. I had
been brought up to be a very strict Muslim. I learned very
quickly that I had to adapt, I had to change otherwise it
wasn't going to work, I wasn't going to be accepted and I
would be isolated... What was really important to me
was my education.*

In 1983 Ayesha succeeded in passing several CSEs (which
was all the school offered) and a GCE 'O' level in English
which she took at a grammar school for visually disabled
boys. Ayesha then went to a further education college for
visually disabled students where she succeeding in passing
more GCE 'O' levels and two GCE 'A' levels. With the help
of a forward thinking careers adviser, Ayesha went to
university in 1986 where she studied social policy and race
relations. She is now completing a PhD degree where she
is investigating the experiences of disabled women from
ethnic minorities.

Ayesha's first job was as a braille proof reader for the
Royal National Institute for the Blind, but after six
months she found employment as a race officer working
with councils and local employers. She then became a
lecturer at her local college of further education teaching
English as a second language and managing a project on
equal opportunities. Ayesha's aim is to become a lecturer
in higher education.

EXPERIENCING DISABILITY

Ayesha's main struggle has been gaining a good education
and this has taken up most of her time. Although she did

experience some racism, she speaks with warmth of her
time in special education:

> There were some good teachers there who pushed me
> on. I was very ignorant of where to go but they saw
> my potential and enthusiasm and they channelled
> me.

At university things were not so easy:

> It was a great struggle. At university they had never
> had a blind student and they took me on a year's
> trial. All the time I had to fight for it; asking for book
> lists in advance, reading things from the board - it
> was constant. I had to be very assertive and they
> didn't like it because they thought I was being really
> awkward and persistent... The course was new so
> there was nothing in braille or on tape. I had to teach
> them, I had to teach the library staff how to help me.
> I had to recruit my own readers... all sorts of things.
> I had no time for a social life, I was working very
> hard, much harder than ever before.

When Ayesha was a child in India she experienced very few
mobility problems even though she had no mobility aid
such as a white stick:

> The environment was very good. I had no mobility
> training, I moved around totally unaided. The village
> was rural so there was no traffic and no roads. There
> was a lot of people and animals. All the houses were
> together in one place and all the land was together in
> another place... of course there were no lamp posts to
> walk into. A couple of times I had a close encounter
> with a snake. I wasn't very much aware of the
> dangers, it was other people who worried.

Ayesha did not feel confined. This was because few people
travelled very far afield,

'Everyone was somewhat confined. People stuck to
their own villages. The adults used to go to other places
on the bus but the children didn't usually go.'

Ayesha uses all forms of modern technology to help her with her studies and her work, for example a scanner that reads print aloud and a computer with voice output. She also uses a guide dog after encouragement from her husband:

> *He thought it would give me more independence - also he loves dogs. But I was frightened of dogs and wasn't sure but I gave it a try and it's worked out well. I wouldn't be without one now.*

Ayesha's main strategy for overcoming disability is one of compensation:

> *I think we have to compensate for disability through achievement and personal development - assertiveness training, personal communication - all of that compensates for the prejudices people might have about you. That's why I'm doing a PhD. I'm working all hours at the moment because it takes much longer. I don't have much life besides doing the PhD but hopefully it is going to be worth it because it is a compensation measure.*

STEPHANIE ARGYRAKIS

Stephanie is thirteen and lives in the South of England with her parents, older sister and younger brother. She has been visually impaired since she was a small baby and her mother is totally blind. Stephanie inherited retinoblastoma, a malignant tumour of the retina. She has one artificial eye and is visually impaired in the other eye. Stephanie finds it particularly difficult to see in sunlight and in the dark.

Stephanie attended a day school for visually disabled children until she was seven but since then has attended mainstream schools. She is in the top stream of her school and achieves high standards in her work. Stephanie has an assistant with her in the classroom for fifteen hours a week to help with any task she cannot see to do such as reading from the blackboard and reading maps. Her mother has fought and won many battles to ensure that Stephanie receives all the help she needs.

Stephanie is a very talented musician. She plays the piano, flute and recorder and has passed advanced examinations in all of these. She has her music enlarged to enable her to see it. Stephanie also enjoys dancing and is a very strong swimmer:

> *I have goggles with my lenses in so that I can see under water. Before I had to wear normal glasses with a band which was really difficult. I found that my swimming improved with the goggles. I can see underwater and I don't bump into people.*

Every year Stephanie goes on holiday with other visually disabled young people who attend mainstream schools. This is paid for by the Social Services department. She enjoys this very much and it has helped to improve her confidence:

> *I thought it was brilliant. I was treated like an adult, I did things that I wouldn't usually do like archery, I did dry slope ski-ing, bowling, trampolining, I liked that, I did athletics and swimming. It showed me that I was not the only person who couldn't do things the way fully sighted people do them. It made me realise that all I can do is my best and not to give up.*

When Stephanie leaves schools she wants to work with young children perhaps in a nursery school. She enjoys the relationship she has with her brother who is six years younger and has spent a lot of time teaching him skills such as playing the piano and how to read and write.

EXPERIENCING DISABILITY

One of the main problems Stephanie experiences as a visually disabled young person is the time it takes her to complete her school work:

Say like some people do half an hour's homework, I'm sometimes doing more than an hour's homework. I have to finish my class work at home. I go to bed a lot later than other people so that I can get through it all. When I first had my end of year exams, I got half way through the geography paper and they told me to finish and they wouldn't give me any extra time even though I explained to them that I wasn't so fast because of my sight. But for the rest of them I had extra time because my Mum got stroppy.

Stephanie is entitled to extra time in all public examinations.

Stephanie frequently has to explain her visual disability to her teachers and does not always get a sympathetic or understanding response. This can cause her some degree of stress:

French is much, much better than last year. Last year it was terrible I had this teacher who never, ever took anything slowly. She didn't understand the problems I had with anything. She always used the board. She was very unsympathetic. I've got a different teacher now and she's really good. Actually I used to cry a lot in French and the first teacher just kind of ignored me but this year I cried once and she really shouted at me...Since then I've come out in the top four in all of the tests.

Stephanie has experienced bullying at school and finds it difficult in some situations to interact with other young people socially:

Everyone's friendly but I don't have many people to go around with at school. In the Summer most of them like to go out in the sun but for me I'd rather stay inside where there's no sun. Last year I had very big trouble, fighting with them, verbally. I got so upset that I was actually saying to my Mum 'I want to go where everyone is the same as me, where everyone knows what it's like.' But now, when I think of it, I don't really think it would be a good option.

Like many young visually disabled people, Stephanie finds her situation embarrassing. She is reluctant to ask for help, especially of her peers, and does not like using a white stick. She related her experiences of mobility training:

> *She came to my school. She was saying that I had to use a symbol cane and I said yes because I thought all you had to do was put it up when you are crossing a road, but I was taught all this stuff about using it along the pavement and to hold it a certain way, I didn't like it at all. I refused to go, I said it was too sunny, that I hated the white stick, and then I started crying and she went...It made me feel embarrassed. I don't want to offend anyone but it made me feel really old, like a granny.*

STRATEGIES FOR OVERCOMING DISABILITY

Stephanie has a classroom assistant to help her at school and uses large print. She also has various visual aids including powerful reading glasses and a monocular for distance vision which she uses to see street numbers and animals in the zoo. Stephanie's mother is very active in helping Stephanie overcome all the barriers she faces both in and out of school, this has not been easy as information from Social Services departments and other organisations is not widely publicised and is not usually available in braille or on tape. The main problem at the present time is ensuring that Stephanie's increasing computer needs are met.

One of Stephanie's major strategies for coping with visual disability is to work for longer hours. This, together with a supportive family and the use of visual aids and human help, has meant that Stephanie has so far coped very well in a mainstream school. Her annual holiday with other visually disabled children, as well as providing great enjoyment, has helped her to become more confident.

SUE AND PAUL NICHOLLS

Sue and Paul Nicholls are a married couple in their forties who have had severe visual impairments from birth. They have two sighted daughters who are now young adults. Sue is now totally blind and Paul has a very small amount of sight which has deteriorated over the years:

> *I don't notice any difference from day to day, it's looking back. I can think back on a time in my life when I could run for a bus without fear of running into a person or a post. But there is no way now that I can walk around my building at work at any great speed.*

Sue and Paul both spent a large part of their childhoods in residential schools for visually disabled children. In most ways they feel let down by the education they received. Paul explained:

> *The schools were too isolated, they set their own very low standards... It's been shown many times with blind and partially sighted people from our generation that they've left school and then gone on and done quite well by their own efforts... On the other hand they did give me a certain amount of independence and I was able to do things on the sporting side that I probably wouldn't have been able to do in an integrated setting.*

Sue went to a commercial college for visually disabled people and trained as a braille shorthand typist. She still works full-time within the clerical field. Paul worked in a factory for some years. He acquired 'O' and 'A' level GCEs through evening study and trained as a teacher but after over 100 unsuccessful applications he gave up the hope of ever finding a teaching post. Instead he worked as an employment officer for the RNIB and now works as a manager for a voluntary organisation.

EXPERIENCING DISABILITY

Sue and Paul identified a large number of barriers in their lives the main ones being connected with information, social interaction and mobility. Regarding information Paul explained:

> *You miss out a lot on the enjoyment of things. It comes back to this information thing. You can enjoy CDs but you can't enjoy choosing them, you can't enjoy reading the sleeve notes so your enjoyment is very much on one level.*

Social interaction was another area which they identified as particularly difficult. This concerned an inability to recognise people, an inability to use non-verbal communication, and difficulty in moving about in unfamiliar settings. These difficulties are compounded by other people's lack of adaptation to their needs:

> **Sue**   *We don't recognise people at all so we are solely dependent on them speaking to us. That is part of the isolation, definitely. You don't know they're there unless they're talking and if they're talking you don't like to interrupt... and not everyone realises that.*
>
> **Paul**   *You can't initiate anything and you can't respond... You don't know who is there. There's no non-verbal communication.*
>
> **Sue**   *And I think other people find that difficult as well, to hold a conversation with you when there is no eye contact and body language.*
>
> **Paul**   *In your own home there is a more equal relationship because you can do things for other people... but when you're in a restaurant or pub you are reliant on other people. You've got to know a place very well before you can even get up and go to the toilet without asking for help. It's a very unequal situation indeed.*

A further difficulty experienced by Sue and Paul is that of mobility. Paul spoke of the problem of pedestrianisation:

> *Old fashioned streets where you had a road and a pavement each side, you knew where you were. Although it might have been quite crowded it was well defined whereas now, in the pedestrianised bit, people walk anywhere, there's no pattern really and the dogs tend to drift. It's more difficult for blind people because they lose some of their clues. The traffic itself was a clue.*

One important area of life where Sue and Paul experienced no particular problems, and where nobody seemed to doubt their ability, was bringing up their children. Sue said:

> *In a way it's an extension of your own life and your own home and that's where you feel capable and secure. We brought up the children as we wanted to, nobody interfered. The most difficult thing was pushing the pram but basically I just walked slowly so that if I did hit anything I didn't hit it very hard.....We always said to them 'Never let us out of your sight' and basically they didn't. I think, on the whole, small children don't want you to be out of their sight. Having the children wasn't a problem, it was under our control and in our own environment, we were not being compared to what other people do either. Whatever we did it was normal to them.*

Strategies for overcoming disability

Sue and Paul both use guide dogs which they find is the best way of getting about safely and efficiently. Sue has always been frightened of dogs but she became a guide dog user a few years ago when the stress of getting about became too great:

> *I felt I was getting more and more tense. I could never enjoy a walk. I felt as if I was getting round shouldered and hunch backed from the stress of it all. It was mainly obstacles in the way, over-hanging hedges, road works and things like that.*

Sue and Paul are both adept at using word processors with voice output but have mixed feelings about the new technology which is now becoming available. Sue explained some of the problems she had experienced at work:

> *The major problem in the first instance was identifying the equipment. Once we had identified it the next problem was to get the Department of Employment to pay for it. Then there were problems with compatibility and the suppliers of some of the equipment didn't know how*

to install it. I didn't have adequate training in the beginning. I've been there for two and a half years now and its only been in the last couple of months that I've got it altogether.

Paul has used a scanner which reads print aloud but he still prefers braille:

It's not such a good alternative to braille... With braille you can decide very quickly whether it is something you want to read, but with the scanner you've got all the trouble of switching it on and even with the best scanner in the world it's still a piece of kit, it's not like reading normally... At least with braille you can do what a sighted person can do, you can identify it quickly and decide whether you want to read it and you can skim down it. The information is much more tangible.

The two major strategies that Sue and Paul identified in overcoming the barriers imposed upon them were the avoidance of difficult situations and seeking help. Paul said:

We avoid or use other people. You get other people to go with you or you simply take the easy way out and get other people to do your shopping for you. In our case if we could find someone we would pay them to do the shopping.

Paul went on to explain that asking for help had become easier as they had become older:

I think as we've got older we feel we've got less to prove. Whereas before I'd walk 100 yards extra to a bus stop where I knew only my bus stopped, now I can't be bothered, I just ask, I don't care... .I don't feel the need to prove things either to myself or other people.

OLWEN MITCHELSON

Olwen was born in the mid-30s and, though she had no personal experiences of visual disability until 1992 when she was in her late 50s, she has been a disabled person for most of her life:

> *When I was little I had pneumonia, I had jaundice, I'd everything going. I was all right until I was married and I had the first child, the first baby boy, and I got rheumatoid arthritis when I was twenty one.*

She had married eighteen months earlier and this was the first of two children. Olwen also had her father-in-law living with them for thirteen years as well as a series of jobs in her 'real full life':

> *After I had my arthritis I had a little job down Chillingham Road, depot clerk for about seven years, and then I was made redundant because they closed it down. And I did a few temporary jobs, until I got back and I worked in American Air Filter, in accounts, on computer. It was lovely. I enjoyed it. Very happy. But then things started going wrong again, with my bones, my bones were brittle. I had my hip replaced. I had to give up work, wasn't fair on other people.*

Until 1992 Olwen had had good eye sight and never needed glasses. In the few years since then, however, the development of her visual impairment has been dramatic. She was told that she had glaucoma and provided with eye drops which were at first effective in improving her eye condition. However, the drops adversely affected her chest and the treatment was stopped, *'I don't understand, one effects the other doesn't it? You take one thing and it makes another worse.'* Her eyes were operated on, though to little effect, and she was informed that cataracts had formed. Later that year, in November, a blood vessel burst in one of her eyes. At that time she was totally blind in one eye and had very little sight in the other. She was told she would be put on a waiting list and, perhaps in a year's time, she would be eligible for an operation, *'It was a terrible Christmas.'* Olwen was operated on, as an emergency, in the February to have a cataract removed, and since then there has been some improvement in her sight.

EXPERIENCING DISABILITY

Olwen's experiences of disability began some forty years before she became visually impaired. The loss of her job, for instance, was through physical disability. Her first encounter with visual disability was during the period of initial diagnosis:

> *'Cos it was an awful shock you know when you lose your eyes, when they told you in such a matter of fact way, that you'd lost your sight, that they couldn't do anything about it and that was it. I was just sent home. I had an awful shock, 'cos I was ill for about a fortnight.*

She sees the attitudes she faced at that time as reflective of expectations and assumptions relating to age:

> *Even though I'm older they were 'at your age what can you expect?' You know they talk to you like that. But you know I'm not old. I'm just 61 and I don't think that's old at all. It's as if to say 'What do you expect at that age?' I'd had enough other problems without losing that.*

Furthermore she was left to her own devices in obtaining relevant information and support in overcoming visual disability. She did eventually obtain formal support, but only through a rather lengthy and convoluted route. One major change was that Olwen could not continue to drive:

> *And my husband when he had his stroke he had to give the car up, so that was two, three years ago. So ever since then we've been stuck without a car, and that's like losing your right arm, isn't it?*

Reading has been a very significant activity for Olwen. Though her sight has improved to the extent that she can now read print, she could not do so during the time when it was most impaired:

> *I couldn't read, and reading something that takes you out of yourself doesn't it? I mean if you get into a book it takes your mind off things. I used to sew a lot but that didn't take your mind off things, like reading.*

STRATEGIES FOR OVERCOMING DISABILITY

Olwen's strategies for overcoming disability have built upon her experiences of disability over many years. One major approach for her has been to learn braille:

> *'I'm enjoying my braille, it's fascinating. It's getting into the nitty-gritty now like. It's getting hard. The shortened versions now I'm into. I know all the alphabet and what not, but it's where they use the 'alm' for 'almost'. The shortened version words, the abbreviations. I'm getting on quite well. I enjoy it.'*

This interest in braille began when Olwen was a Brownie and then as a Guide. The library service is also a form of support which she talks about with enthusiasm:

> *They just ask you at the beginning what sort of things you like to read. And then they bring a variety. They bring a lot of mysteries which I don't mind... you put up with the good and the bad don't you?*

JOAN WILSON

> *'Well, in 1990 I went to the opticians. 'Cos I've never had good sight, but I've always had very good close sight. This is what I can't understand. I went to the opticians because I thought I wasn't seeing so well, and he discovered a shadow on this eye.'*

Joan was 68. Her story, then, is one in which visual disability had no personal significance for many years. She spent her 'very happy childhood' as one of six children in 'rather a poor family', brought up by her widowed mother and attending a Catholic school where she became head girl. At fourteen, kitted out in a new apron and cap, she was taken to work in a canning factory, 'The clanging of the machines, it was dramatic for a fourteen year old to do that.' She had a series of jobs during her working life ranging from being a welder during the war to a job as a cashier and receptionist for *Rediffusion* from which she retired with a small pension in 1982.

Joan married at the end of the war when her husband-to-be returned from Burma. Their first child, a girl, was born within a couple of years, but there was then a thirteen year gap before the birth of her son. They now have two granddaughters, the youngest being only four years old. When they were first married the Wilsons rented a small flat quite close to Joan's mother whose health was poor. They lived there until 1976, caring for her until she died, when they moved into their first council house.

After her visit to the opticians in 1990, Joan had to wait nine months for an appointment at the infirmary. She was then told that she had macula degeneration affecting her left eye, but he said *'well you're all right with the other eye so just carry on.'*

EXPERIENCING DISABILITY

And it was 1993 when I was reading a book, which I had been reading, small print, newspapers and everything, and I saw a little blob on the paper.

Joan remembers her experiences at this time as demeaning and disabling. Having had thirty photographs taken of her eyes she returned for the diagnosis:

> *When I went back for the negatives, oh it was terrible. He lifted them up to the light and he said to the nurse 'Macula degeneration in both eyes, sign a BDS form' or whatever it is. And then he turned to me and he said 'There's nothing we can do about it.' He said 'You'll always be able to see sideways, but you've got no central vision.'... So I came home very, very upset about it.*

This first encounter with visual disability was a dramatic and significant experience:

> *I think when you're diagnosed, at the beginning like at the infirmary. I shouldn't have been told like that, it should have been explained to me then what it entailed, and what I had to look forward to, you know. It was so abrupt the introduction to it. And it was just shot at you without any feeling at all.*

At this point Joan was given only a medical diagnosis and the feeling that she was 'just wiped off':

> *The lack of information in the beginning was very, very poor... I had to do it myself.*

Reflecting on day-to-day living, Joan talked first of the social experiences of visual disability:

> *When I go out I don't know whether I'm passing someone I know or not, unless they speak to me. And I feel shut off a bit, I feel isolated by that. Because I used to go along that path and people used to say 'Hello, Hello there' you know. Now I go passed and nobody... it's a feeling of isolation... I've lost all my social life. I've lost all that, apart from my family.*

She now never leaves the house unless with her husband, daughter or other member of the family. Shopping, including window shopping, was an activity that Joan enjoyed, but it is now a different experience:

> *My poor husband. He's so patient with me and I get so frustrated in the shops, because I can't make out any labels. I can't make out any prices... And I come home and he's picked up all the wrong things.*

Since childhood Joan's main leisure activities have been of the needlework and handicraft type. She wouldn't sit down to watch the television without her knitting, always to complex patterns. She has now 'comes down to' knitting squares for blankets for *Oxfam*, and finding increasingly that she is bored.

STRATEGIES FOR OVERCOMING DISABILITY

And one day I said 'oh I'm going to ring the social services and see if they can do anything for me.' So I rang the social services and they put me on to G... she got me a talking book machine which was great, because I missed my books, you see I was a reader.

Over the past couple of years, Joan has introduced a good number of adaptations to her home. These include adaptations to the cooker, and acquiring new appliances, such as a talking microwave oven and talking scales. Adaptations have been made, too, to activities. Joan now, for instance, records and exchanges audio-tapes with her sister who lives abroad, rather than writing.

A major source of support has been a local self-help group:

> *G... said she'd formed a little club... so I went along thinking if I can get any help from people there in the same position as myself it will be a good thing... and it is good because we are all suffering some form of visual loss.*

Joan's family has also provided support, particularly her husband. There are dilemmas in this, however. The support which Joan feels she needs also, at times, makes her feel dependent:

> *And he takes me out in the car. But I worry that I'm losing my independence, you know what I mean. I've been very independent all my life and I feel that I'm losing it. And I got a bit distressed about that you know.*

ALAN DUDLEY

Alan is a 46 year old social worker and this case study concentrates on his experiences in his career. He began by telling us:

Totally blind, no light perception, nothing. Since birth, my visual impairment's caused by being a premature baby. Now, I was in an oxygen tent for six weeks and

*therefore lost my sight through that. Education... went to
special schools from the age of five... and I took 'O' levels
at school, got six. I was trained as an audio/shorthand
typist, and I left there at the age of 20, pushing 21 with
the idea that I would be a typist... which I hated.*

He only lasted as a typist for three years and, following
some voluntary work he trained and qualified in 1977 as a
social worker in Newcastle. Having obtained a post he
worked first in child-care, then as a specialist social worker
for visually disabled people, and is now a Team Leader in
charge of a generic social work team.

EXPERIENCING DISABILITY

I suppose the first barrier was trying to get on a course.

He wrote to and was refused by ten training
institutions. He had the same problem getting a first post
once he had qualified. He puts this down to sighted
people's beliefs that he couldn't do the job:

*There were concerns about situations they were putting
me in, whether there were dangers to me and whether I
was at risk. There were concerns about how I perceive
situations when I have no sight. Would I pick up
nuances and subtleties? Would I be able to describe
situations accurately because of that? Practical things
like would I be able get to the houses and so forth,
would I get there and back? Situations like, how would
I deal with it if I got threatened, or even attacked, and
would they somehow be to blame for that?*

Alongside this Alan cites his own lack of confidence in
himself:

*I think also, barriers you have considering yourself.
You have your own doubts whether you can manage
this. They're going to send you to some street, are you
going to be able to find it? And how are you going to
cope when you get into the house and you experience
hostility? Or are people going to do things behind
your back? Or are you going to miss things?*

After being in post for a while, some people continued to doubt his capabilities solely on the basis of his blindness:

Instead of asking how I coped with it, and I think I did, they just decided that I couldn't. So, if you can't see, you can't do it.

There were other presumptions that had angered Alan:

> *They thought that if you're blind, you'd know a lot about blindness, which may or may not be true, and that therefore you'd be able to make a significant difference. And they find it very difficult to accept that it might not be so, or that I didn't want it to be so.*

Barriers to written information has proved to be the main practical problem.

STRATEGIES FOR OVERCOMING DISABILITY

Alan's main route to overcoming barriers has been through reciprocity in helping and working relationships. Whilst in training, his fellow students, for instance, would help Alan search the literature, 'But I could make contributions 'cos there were subjects that I was apparently quite good at, and they weren't so hot on, so I could make contributions by explaining things.' This also happens in his work with colleagues:

> *People regard you as part of the office, part of the scene, because they'll come and they'll say, 'What about this Alan, I'm really worried about this, can you help?' And I would contribute to their work, and I would go with them. So it became a reciprocity, I suppose.*

Alan also feels that he overcomes barriers through his personality, and particularly his sense of humour:

And I guess you can either sit on your bottom and cry about it or say 'well I'll have to get on with this world somehow', and I've tended to want to get on with the world. And so when things happen at work that could be construed as discriminatory, or people being totally

*unaware, I've tended to laugh at them because it's so
funny.*

He believes in being pragmatic about his need for help:

*I mean I live independently, but I'm dependent on
people. I'm dependent on Mrs. Brown at the bus stop
saying, 'There's a number 57 coming.' I'm dependent
on the bus driver to some extent, particularly new
areas saying, 'Here's the bus stop mate'... You're
dependent on shop-assistants giving you a hand in
shops, selling you decent clothes.*

And he believes in recognising the viewpoint of helpers:
*People are cautious, careful, wary, worried, anxious,
uncertain about what they are going to do to assist you.*

He has developed many practical strategies, including
using a guide dog, braille and personal assistants as
readers. He also has ways of working with clients and
colleagues, for instance:

*And so you get to the house door, and I always step
back from the door once I've rung the bell, so that I'm
a couple of paces away from the door. Always make
sure the dog's sitting, so that the dog's not imposing
itself on them. And then, they answer the door, you
usually put out your hand, I find that a good start, I
like to touch people, in that sense.*

Our analysis within these case studies has illustrated the
barriers experienced by visually disabled people and their
strategies for overcoming them. Alan, however, also feels
that blindness can be of benefit to him in his work:
*I have this theory that it (blindness) somehow
smoothes or levels out the relationship a little. Because
when you go in there as a professional you are also
seeking help from the person, then they are able to offer
you something back. And I think from time to time in my
work that has helped.*

In practice

RE-CONCEIVING SOCIAL SUPPORT

There is little doubt that visually disabled people experience a range of emotions such as irritation, frustration and distress, associated with their lack or loss of vision. It has, in the past, been common practice for social workers and other professionals to view 'problems' of visual disability as residing within the individual. Intervention has therefore centred around counselling individuals in order to help them 'come to terms' with their loss of vision and to adjust their lifestyles and expectations accordingly. Services for visually disabled people have centred around the discourse of 'rehabilitation' in which disabled people are expected to learn new skills and strategies to maintain personal and economic self reliance. Failure to comply with such interventions may have resulted in the individual being labelled as unresponsive, or not amenable to 'help', thus further pathologising the individual.

Today, many social workers and other professionals prefer to view visual disability through a different lens; as socially constructed barriers to education, transport, employment, and leisure. This represents a move towards the social model of disability, as discussed in Section 1, and the form of analysis adopted in Section 2, that is in terms of disabling barriers experienced by disabled people. From this perspective, it is not the visually disabled person who must change, but non-disabled people, their organisations and institutions. As a consequence professionals have had to learn new skills in order to work in partnership with disabled people to overcome discrimination and oppression, and to campaign for citizenship and rights.

However there is a tension between the social model of disability and the practical and emotional needs of visually disabled people and care must be taken not to throw the baby out with the bath water! Cynical interpretation of the social model of disability, by those wishing to cut back on state welfare provision, may well appear to support cuts in existing resources on the basis of a rejection of the 'nanny state'. The final part of this guide addresses issues of professional practice as they are informed by the social model of disability.

THE CONTEXT OF SERVICES AND RESOURCES

In the past thirty years, statutory services and resources for visually disabled people have been eroded. Legislation such as the Chronically Sick and Disabled Persons Act (1970) and the NHS and Community Care Act (1990) has removed the right of visually disabled people to statutory representation (Williams 1993). Local authorities no longer have a statutory responsibility to visit newly registered blind or partially sighted people. Services and resources are no longer a right but are provided at the discretion of a Care Manager who has the imperative to target services on those in greatest need. Recent reports detail the low priority afforded to visually disabled people by Social Services departments as well as poor practice, weak inter-agency collaboration at the registration stage, and inadequate or inappropriate services (Lovelock et al 1995, James and Thomas 1996). In addition, NHS cutbacks have resulted in patients having to wait longer for appointments with ophthalmologists. This point was made by Joan Wilson who told us that she waited nine months to see the ophthalmologist:

> ...and when I went to see the consultant he looked at this eye and he said '...well we can't do nothing about this. If you had come here earlier we might have been able to use a laser' ...and I came home and told my husband and he said 'well why didn't you tell them you'd been waiting nine months?' And I said that my speech was taken away from me when he said he couldn't do nothing with the eye.

Despite the recommendations contained in several recent reports (DoH 1989, Social Services Inspectorate 1991, Williams 1993) that information, counselling and support

for visually disabled people should be available at the
point of diagnosis at the hospital, in reality very few eye
departments offer such a service. Williams (1993)
observes that consultations with ophthalmologists last, on
average, between three and five minutes, which obviously
does not allow patients time to ask for information about
their eye conditions, let alone enable them to consider
their social support needs.

Bruce et al (1991) found that only 17% of newly
registered people had been visited at the time or shortly
after certification. Neither Joan nor Olwen were given any
information at the hospital about what services or
resources might be available to them. Olwen told us:

> *...It's just knowing who to contact and where to go if
> anything happens like this. I mean if they give you
> this information (at the beginning) it would be a lot
> easier.*

Joan had a similar experience. She was sent some
information through the post but was expected to initiate
contact with social services if she felt the need:

> *I had to do it myself. There was no information about
> who you could go to. It was a few weeks before I sat
> down and thought 'well social services might have
> something to help me.'*

Practitioners wishing to implement the social model of
disability might begin by investigating the sources of
information and support available to newly diagnosed and
registered visually disabled people in their own area. The
social model requires professionals to widen the target for
change from the 'individual' client to non-disabled people
and their organisations. Identifying and challenging
shortfalls in essential services for visually disabled people
is therefore perceived as a legitimate form of intervention.

Williams (1993) suggests that the separation of
'specialist' services for visually disabled people from the
mainstream social services provision has had an impact
upon the views of generic social workers about working

with visually disabled people and upon the isolation of 'specialist' workers. She goes on to say that:

> *The word 'blind' seems to induce a 'switching off'*
> *mechanism for some SSD staff. Typical remarks are,*
> *'This is not my area of work' or 'Work with 'the blind'*
> *is best done by specialists.'*
>
> *(1993:45)*

Such attitudes of non-specialist workers can result in ignorance or disinterest in the sources of support for visually disabled people. In addition, it can also mean that visual disability is overlooked by care managers assessing the needs of older people, children and people with learning difficulties (Williams 1993). James and Thomas argue:

> *Visual disability occurs in all groups in society… This*
> *suggests that all social workers should undergo some*
> *basic instruction on work with visually disabled*
> *people. The case is stronger still for those choosing to*
> *work with old people or where care management is*
> *the intended career.*
>
> *(1996:37)*

It is therefore the responsibility of all social workers, and not just those who specialise in this area of work, that organisations such as hospitals and social services departments respond appropriately to the information and support needs of this marginalised and neglected group of consumers.

Williams (1993) argues that primary health care workers have a lack of knowledge and understanding of visual disability issues. For example, Olwen tried to talk to the practice nurse about her visual impairment but found that the nurse seemed unable to understand or respond to her needs:

> *…the social services didn't know what I wanted. That*
> *was the problem when I got talking to the nurse from the*
> *Doctor's. She didn't understand what I wanted.*

The Social Services Inspectorate (1988) found that specialist services, workers and visually disabled people themselves are frequently marginalised within Social Services departments and that the present training for specialist workers emphasises the practical and rehabilitative aspects of work with visually disabled people but lacks a well articulated knowledge base. The number of specialist workers employed by Social Services departments, such as mobility officers and rehabilitation workers, have been falling and James and Thomas (1996) suggest that the work is perceived as being of low status and lacking in career opportunities.

The introduction of legislation such as the NHS and Community Care Act (1990) has reinforced the idea that services are provided on the basis of the 'professional' assessment of needs rather than civil rights, and visually disabled people appear to have little priority in the current methods of distribution of these scarce resources and very few allies within the social work profession. The marginalisaton of specialist workers and the decline in services and sources of social support indicate that visual disability has dropped off the agenda of most social workers. This guide attempts to reinstate visual disability issues as a legitimate area of concern and action for all social workers and other practitioners.

Professional practice with visually disabled people seems firmly rooted in the medical model of disability - for example, it is the only form of impairment that requires medical certification before registration. Specialist services for visually disabled people are embedded in the discourse of rehabilitation. Finkelstein and Stuart comment:

> *Over time the medical model crystallised in the philosophy of 'rehabilitation' and its enabling legislation and this still remains one of the key reference points for current services.*
>
> ***(1996:184)***

Barnes (1996) makes the point that while medical interventions may well be appropriate for minimising and monitoring the negative effects of impairment, they are inappropriate for dealing with disability:

Professionals working within this perspective invariably pathologise the experience of impairment and

in so doing compound the problems faced by disabled
people; directing us into segregated special schools and
sheltered workshops are two good examples.

Barnes (1996:43)

Thompson (1993) suggests that anti-discriminatory (social
work) practice must aim for a de-medicalisation of social
work and embrace a more critical model of disability. To
treat disabled people as if they were ill or in need of
medical supervision is dehumanising and oppressive. One
of the authors has recently been registered blind and has
sought the services of a mobility officer to teach her to use
the long cane. However, before this training could begin,
the mobility officer was obliged to seek the approval of
the GP.

The idea that disabled people are 'needy' while non-
disabled people are not, is part of the dominant disablist
discourse. Failure to recognise the fact that all people rely
on assistance, such as the postal system and public
transport, and that the assistance that disabled people
need is not 'special' but different, is both oppressive and
divisive (Finkelstein and Stuart 1996, Thompson 1993).
From the perspective of the social model of disability, then,
the services for visually disabled people should be based
on the principle of rights rather than 'care or cure'
(Finkelstein and Stuart 1996) and professionals should be
a source of social support for achieving a desired lifestyle.

BARRIERS TO CHANGING PRACTICE

It is important for practitioners to reflect upon their own
prejudices and assumptions and think how they might
impact upon their practice with visually disabled clients, or
their relations with visually disabled colleagues. Such
reflections challenge forms of communication and
procedures in their own agencies that exclude or
marginalise visually disabled people.

Practitioners can also reflect upon their favourite
theories/models/practices and examine them for their
potential to marginalise or disadvantage visually disabled
people. From the perspective of the social model of
disability, models such as assertiveness training, self
advocacy and facilitating self help may be more

appropriate than those models that focus upon promoting individual adjustment to impairment and rehabilitation. In addition, the social model requires professionals to intervene at a structural and organisational level to challenge the disabling barriers that prevent visually disabled people from participating fully in society.

INFORMAL THEORIES

Professionals who do not have frequent contact with visually disabled people may need to be aware of some of the common misconceptions associated with visual impairment. Many of these misconceptions are rooted in the medical/individual model of disability; they compound and maintain oppression and prevent visually disabled people from taking part in mainstream society. Belief in such misconceptions is not restricted to sighted people: some visually disabled people may need this information too. Many have spent a large part of their lives as sighted people and may therefore, have the same misconceptions of blindness. Common misconceptions are:

a   That blind people see absolutely nothing. This is not true. Only a very small percentage of registered blind people have no vision whatsoever. The vast majority of people retain some useful vision; even the distinction between light and dark allows people to orientate themselves in a room. Alan, a visually disabled social worker, explained:

> *'I think with the professionals, and this goes for some social workers too, when confronted with someone with poor sight, or no sight at all, they immediately have stereotypical images. That you live in a world of darkness for example... I was in (a local department store) once and I went to buy a light bulb and she said to me 'Why do you need light bulbs in your house?'*

The statutory definition of blindness is '...so blind as to be unable to perform any work for which eyesight is essential.' Whilst the guidelines for registration of partial sight advise '...that a person be certified as partially sighted if they are substantially and permanently handicapped by defective vision caused by congenital defect, illness, or injury.' **(Cited in Williams 1993)**

b That the vision of visually disabled individuals is constant under all conditions. This is not so. Some eye conditions mean that individuals can see to get around in daylight but lose their vision at night. With others, the opposite is the case; they cannot see in bright sunlight but can see at dusk or in the dark. Others have eye conditions which mean that their vision can change from day to day.

These issues underline the need for social workers to listen to visually disabled people and recognise their expert knowledge about the effects of their impairment on their functioning and their subsequent needs and wants. This has implications for such issues as where and at what time of day assessments of mobility should be undertaken. Paying careful attention to users' descriptions of how their impairments affects them can avoid oppressive assumptions that day to day variations in mobility and dexterity mean that they are lying or exaggerating.

c That visually disabled people cannot read print. While it may be the case that some cannot, the vast majority can read print in some form or under certain light conditions. Some people may be registered partially sighted because they experience tunnel vision. In this case, they may have useful central vision which will allow them to read normally. Such complexities can lead to misunderstandings. For example, a visually disabled person might be seen reading in a bus or a train but when they get off, they may ask for assistance to cross the road. Lack of understanding may lead to disbelief that the person is visually disabled, and help may be refused. Similarly, non-disabled people may assume that if a person can see to read, he or she should also be able to recognise people in the street. This is not necessarily so and visually disabled people are often regarded as unfriendly or moody when they do not acknowledge people. This problem was highlighted in the case studies of Sue and Paul and Joan.

d That visually disabled people develop a sixth sense to compensate for their lack of vision. This is not so. The stress and anxiety associated with getting about safely may mean that visually impaired people use all their powers of concentration when out and about but their other senses are not superior to those of sighted people.

e   It is a common misconception that if visually disabled people
    try to use their residual vision they may accelerate deterioration
    of their vision. This is not the case.
    However, they may experience headaches or muscle fatigue
    associated with the effort of using their residual vision. This
    particular misconception was associated with the damaging
    policies of 'saving' sight which were prevalent until the
    Second World War, such as the creation of 'sight saving'
    schools, and the policy of making all visually disabled children
    use Braille   (Corley 1989).

All of these misconceptions feed prejudice and maintain the
social barriers that prevent visually disabled people from
participating fully in mainstream society. Professionals
need to be aware of their own prejudice and stereotypical
assumptions about visual disability and to reflect upon
how such assumptions shape their professional practice.

FORMAL THEORIES

Formal theories and their discursive practices may also
need to be deconstructed in the light of the social model
of disability. One example is the notion that theories of
grief and loss and the associated practices of grief
counselling, can be transferred to work with those who
have lost their sight. Whilst it is acknowledged that loss of
vision can be very upsetting for the individual and that
some people may benefit from counselling, there is
nevertheless, a danger that such theories may be used in
an instrumental fashion and without the agreement of the
person concerned. Oliver (1983) gives the example of a
newly blinded woman who was told she could not have
adjusted because she was not depressed enough.

   Professionals should be aware of forms of
communication that may exclude or marginalise visually
disabled people. For example, some theories and models
of professional practice, such as group work, rely heavily
upon non-verbal communication, both as forms of
assessment and intervention. Models of practice can be
adapted so that they are not oppressive to visually disabled
people. A starting point for a group leader is to ask the
visually disabled member what would be helpful and adapt
the proceedings accordingly.

Taken-for-granted procedures and processes within professional agencies can exclude and marginalise visually disabled clients and staff. For example, case conferences, where permission to contribute to the discussion is sought by catching the Chair's eye, or indicating with a hand movement, can effectively silence visually disabled people. Such silencing is compounded by the power imbalances in such meetings when the visually disabled person is a user among a host of professionals. Similar difficulties arise when written material is expected to be read during a meeting. Both of these examples serve to illustrate that social work agencies, along with other welfare organisations, are organised by and for sighted people. Many visually disabled professionals have developed strategies to deal with such discrimination. Alan explains that:

'I chair meetings with families of service users and you have to say 'right folks, I don't have any sight so when we start the meeting, if you want to say something, don't raise your hand, don't catch my eye, don't raise your eyebrows, speak... It's their responsibility to give me a shout. Most people do.'

However, many social work agencies expect visually disabled people to adapt to their inaccessible procedures and information and perceive any difficulties that may arise as a personal failing of the visually disabled person. For example, Alan found that:

...the major problem is reading files, reading post, reading the new referrals that come in every day. Writing on new referrals what is to be done. So they are the major barriers... you can be seen as inefficient, always demanding. I've had rows with people at times about this... because they think of the world as a sighted place. They don't understand that for me, a pile of papers is just a pile of blank sheets. Therefore they sometimes characterise me as being inefficient and I'll say 'you're judging me by sighted people's rules and I refuse to be judged by that.'

WORKING IN PARTNERSHIP

Oliver (1996) argues that the structure of welfare services puts the power and control of those services in the hands of the professionals. Professionals operating within the strictures of the NHS and Community Care Act control the provision of scarce resources to visually disabled people through the process of assessment (Lovelock et al 1995). Despite the rhetoric of 'needs-led' assessment, a disabled person's needs will continue to be reframed to fit budget constraints and the local availability of social support. Assessment of needs is an exercise in power. Research has shown that professional assessment of needs often misrepresents or even distorts or denies the needs of disabled people (Oliver 1996).

While professionals may well feel constrained by their agency role or the administrative procedures required in carrying out an assessment, there usually remains some degree of flexibility in which professionals can look for opportunities to work in partnership with visually disabled people. For example, professionals can share power by sharing 'expert' knowledge and information. Many visually disabled people complain that they have not been given an adequate explanation about their impairment and prognosis. Others say that professionals use jargon or medical terminology that is unintelligible to the lay person. Information about services and resources should also be in an accessible form for visually disabled people. The vast majority of registered people do not use braille or moon but prefer to rely upon print. Four out of five visually disabled people can read large print and many can read print of a standard size. Practitioners should examine their own information sources for users for evidence of discrimination against visually disabled people. Raising the awareness of those who produce leaflets, forms and so on within their own agencies is a legitimate role for professionals working within a social model of disability.

Another major source of information for visually disabled people is other people. Other people may well be accessed by telephone or by listening to radio or television. Many people seeking information try to do so by telephone. A rehabilitation worker employed by a Social Services department told one of us that, in her experience, administrative and reception staff are not aware of the sources of social support for visually disabled people and she had many examples of clients being turned away or given incorrect information. Social Service Departments and other welfare organisations have a responsibility to ensure that front-line staff, such as receptionists and secretaries, have the opportunity to undertake disability equality training and are also provided with accurate information about the sources of social support for visually disabled people.

Another way of working in partnership is by recognising and acknowledging the visually disabled person's expertise in relation to the meaning and experience of being visually disabled. This means encouraging people to exercise choice of services appropriate to their desired lifestyles, thus avoiding what Williams (1993) refers to as the 'white stick and talking book' response, the kind of response Stephanie experienced in mobility training. At a wider level, the expertise of visually disabled people should be allowed to influence the development of services. However, Finkelstein and Stuart observe that:

> *Disabled people and their organisations are still almost completely absent from any real decision making in the planning and delivery of services or public utilities that they may use... Information about appropriate services then, arising out of the experience and perspective of disabled peoples' lifestyles is very limited*
>
> ***(1996:171)***

From the perspective of the social model of disability, professional power should be used to highlight the shortfall in resources for visually disabled people; to ensure that the subjugated voices of visually disabled people are heard and responded to and to encourage and support people to assert themselves so that their expertise about visual disability is at the centre of the development of services and support.

It is important that practitioners make a conscious decision to heighten their awareness of visual disability as an area of inquiry in all social work assessments. Visual disability has implications for good practice in terns of professionals finding methods of written and verbal communication that are accessible to the user. Visual disability may not be the major focus of professional intervention but ignoring it may seriously inhibit the possibilities of working in partnership.

Practitioners can share power with visually disabled people by sharing expertise and information. For example, they can use their expertise to research possible sources of support so that users can make informed choices. Practitioners can also encourage clients to actively participate in the writing of reports and case files so that their voices are heard and their views represented in 'official' documents. They can empower users by encouraging then to take part in drawing up criteria for recruiting personal help.

Finally, working in partnership means actively recognising and respecting the 'expertise' of users in relation to how they experience disability and their views on what they want and need. Practitioners can work in partnership with visually disabled people by seeing themselves as a resource (expertise, information, advocacy) so that users can work towards achieving their desired lifestyles. Practitioners may like to adopt the following procedure:

- Clarify the goals towards which the person aspires
- Identify the barriers which may prevent the realisation of these goals.
- Work toward removing the barriers.

Professionals can actively encourage visually disabled people to become involved in forums where they can influence the development of relevant services. This includes ensuring that meetings are held in accessible venues and that visually disabled people are not excluded by lack of transport or inappropriate mediums of communication. Visually disabled people appreciate receiving minutes of meetings and reports in advance, something they have in common with many sighted people but which may, for them, be the only way of successfully accessing the information.

Assessments by professionals should include some questions about a person's vision and the barriers they experience. They should provide a basis for responding appropriately to the communication and information needs of anyone with a sight loss. Many visually disabled people have learned ways of concealing or denying their visual loss because of the prejudice they have experienced in the past. It is not always possible or appropriate to hand over the case to a specialist worker; especially when the reason for referral is not associated with the person's visual disability (for example a child protection or mental health issue).

ANTI-DISCRIMINATORY AND ANTI-OPPRESSIVE PRACTICE

Thompson (1993) makes the following distinction between discrimination and oppression. Discrimination is:

> *The unfair or unequal treatment of individuals or groups... who characteristically belong to relatively powerless groups within the social structure. Oppression (is the) inhuman or degrading treatment of individuals or groups... brought about by the dominance of one group over another; the negative and demeaning exercise of power. Oppression often involves disregarding the rights of an individual or group and is thus a denial of citizenship.*
>
> *(1993:31)*

As Thompson (1993) points out, professionals have a great deal of power over those who consult them and there are many circumstances in which the exercise of professional power can be experienced as discriminatory or oppressive. Anti-discriminatory practice is therefore concerned with combating misuses of power by professionals and their agencies as well as urging professionals to challenge the practices of others.

Visually disabled people experience discrimination in many areas of their lives for example in employment (Bruce et al 1991). There is a commonly held belief that there are a large number of visually disabled people employed as social workers. In fact, along with disabled people in general, the numbers employed or accepted onto Dip SW programmes is disgracefully low (Baron et al 1996, James and Thomas 1996). Alan had ten rejections before he was finally offered a place on a course. Once qualified, he had similar difficulties in obtaining a job:

> *I was told by many local authorities 'well if you want to work with blind people we'll offer you a job, but if you don't, we're not prepared to.' I can actually remember crying tears of frustration over this issue.*

Ian, another visually disabled social worker we interviewed, had a similar experience. He went for an interview for a generic social work post and:

> *...they offered me the opportunity of becoming their social worker for the blind...which I desperately didn't want because one of the reasons for leaving N was that I wanted to get away from the feeling within me, and within everybody else, that all I could do is work with the blind.*

Once in employment, both Alan and Ian experienced discrimination at the hands of their colleagues. For example, Ian found that he had to convince his colleagues that he could do the job:

> *They expected that I wouldn't be able to do reports and I wouldn't be able to find my way about... They concentrated an awful lot on the fact that I wouldn't be able to see what people looked like. I deliberately took every opportunity I could to volunteer for intake duties to prove to them that I could actually do it... I was always taught 'you don't have to be as good as, you have to be better and if you're not better you won't get there.'*

Alan told of how he had experienced discrimination at the hands of his line manager when the manager made assumptions that Alan was unable, because of his visual disability, to work with a non-accidental injury case:

> *We had quite a lot of success with him and when I came to close the case, my senior felt that it shouldn't be closed. My senior felt that... as there had been a non-accidental injury in the case eighteen months previous, I shouldn't have that case. Didn't discuss it with me, just took it off me... Instead of asking how I coped with it, and I think I did, they just decided that I couldn't. If you can't see, you can't do it.*

Baron et al (1996) found similar examples of visually disabled social workers experiencing discrimination. One student, who had successfully completed her social work training:

> *...encountered an explicit debate about the possibility of her achieving professional competence. Could a visually impaired student properly work in offenders' services where, for example, she might be required to identify witnesses in court?*   *(1996:368)*

Discrimination is also to be found in education. Ayesha's account describes some of the barriers she faced as a university student. Baron et al (1996) found that there were many disabling barriers to recruitment and training on Dip SW programmes:

> *A lack of experience of disability issues was evident as well as the absence of an active approach to arrange support at all levels of the programme...*
>
> *(1996:175)*

One of our colleagues told of how a visually disabled student, who was undertaking a Diploma in Social Work, was expected, by the University, to apply to the 'hardship' fund for a grant to pay for the brailling of course handouts: handouts which other, non-disabled, students were given free. This particular student successfully completed her training two years ago and has been unsuccessful in securing an appointment as a qualified worker. She has recently taken a job in a Day Centre which does not require a professional qualification and is receiving a salary much below that of a qualified social worker.

James and Thomas (1996) undertook a project to give greater prominence to work with visually disabled people on a Diploma in Social Work Course and to attract more visually disabled students to social work training. They found that many practice teachers in voluntary and statutory settings were reluctant to take on visually disabled students and cited fire regulations, or the fear that they would be vulnerable to violent and aggressive clients as justifications. They go on to say:

> *Some practice teachers... felt very strongly that a blind student could not function effectively in the child care field... Others had anxieties around work with mentally ill people... In effect, visually disabled students had to prove themselves competent in a manner which would not have been expected of non-disabled students in similar circumstances.*
>
> *(1996:41-42)*

It is clear that discrimination and oppression occurs (albeit sometimes unintentionally or unconsciously) within professionals' own agencies and is embedded within such everyday practices as student training and recruitment.

Professionals' anti-discriminatory practice with those who consult them should involve close scrutiny of equality in issues such as access to buildings, services, resources and information for visually disabled people. Such awareness can be encouraged and developed through disability equality training, which is run by highly trained disabled people. Disability equality training:

> *...is primarily about changing the meaning of disability from individual tragedy to social oppression; it emphasises the politics of disability, the social and physical barriers that disabled people face, and the links with other oppressed groups.*
>
> *(French 1996:121)*

This is in contrast to disability awareness training which attempts to facilitate awareness in non-disabled people of what it is like to be disabled. Such training is characterised by simulation exercises in which non-disabled people are required to use wheelchairs or wear blindfolds in the hope that this will help them understand the experiences of disabled people. Such training has been criticised by those who adhere to the social model of disability (Swain and Lawrence 1994) on the grounds that it concentrates on individual impairment rather than disabling barriers; that it ignores the fact that disabled people develop skills and strategies, which the blindfolded non-disabled person would not possess; and there is little evidence to suggest that it changes attitudes (French 1996).

Professionals need to consider how they and their agencies respond to those people who belong to more than one oppressed group. As we have discussed earlier, many visually disabled people are elderly and experience the simultaneous oppressions of ageism and disablism. For example, there is evidence to suggest that elderly people are given low priority in relation to mobility training (Bruce et al 1991), based on the ageist assumption that elderly people don't get out and about very much.

Stuart describes three ways in which black disabled people experience multiple oppression:

> *...first, limited or no individuality or identity; second, resource discrimination; finally, isolation within black communities and the family.... In sum, they isolate black disabled people and place them at the margins of the ethnic minority and disabled populations.*
>
> *(1993:95)*

Williams (1993) makes the point that black people are under-represented among those who are registered visually disabled, yet there is anecdotal evidence to suggest that there is actually a higher incidence of visual disability among ethnic minority groups. She suggests that Social Services departments and Health Authorities should ensure that:

> *...Information is accessible in appropriate languages, as well as appropriate formats; cultural differences are respected and taken into account; and that interpreters are available.*
>
> **(1993:54)**

The helper/helped relationship between visually disabled people and professionals needs to be deconstructed in relation to its potential for maintaining the stereotypical image of disabled people as passive and pitiful. In the last decade, the concept of 'empowerment' has emerged as a means of addressing the inequalities of power between professionals and their clients. However, as Oliver (1996) suggests, the concept is not without its problems:

> *The general view of empowerment is that those with power will give some of that power to those who have little or no power. Empowerment is in the gift of the empowerer. It is further assumed that professionals, by the development of certain practices, can empower their clients.*
>
> *(1996:147)*

Anti-oppressive practice requires professionals to move away from the traditional casework approach to 'helping' and to work with a much broader brief. In partnership with disabled people's organisations and the self help movement, such professionals can intervene at the level of organisation and community to further the fight for citizenship and rights of visually disabled people.

Conclusion

In this guide we have attempted to link theory about visual disability with professional practice and have shown that visually disabled people, like all disabled people, experience oppression in many aspects of their lives including interaction with professionals. We hope that this guide will give social workers and other professionals help and ideas on the many ways in which visually disabled people may be assisted. The lifestyles and experiences of visually disabled people, as we have seen, are very diverse with every person being a unique individual with specific aspirations, needs and goals. It is not possible to learn 'all about visual disability' from a guide such as this, but we hope it has stimulated you to find out more; talking to visually disabled people and respecting their expertise is a most valuable source of information and learning. Visually disabled people are, however, part of the wider community of disabled people and much can be learned by exploring all aspects of disability from a civil rights perspective.

References

Barnes C. (1993) *Disabling Imagery and the Media: an exploration of the principles for media representations of disabled people.* Ryburn. Halifax.

Barnes C. (1996) Visual Impairment and Disability. In Hales G. (ed.) *Beyond Disability: towards an enabling society.* Sage. London.

Baron S., Phillips R., and Stalker K. (1996) Barriers to training for disabled social work students. *Disability and Society* 11 (3) 361-377.

Begum N. (1994) Mirror, Mirror on the Wall. In Begum N., Hill M. and Stevens A. (eds.) *Reflections: views of black disabled people on their lives and community care.* Central Council of Education and Training in Social Work. Paper 32.3 London.

Begum N., Hill M. and Stevens A. (1994) *Reflections: views of black disabled people on their lives and community care.* Central Council of Education and Training in Social Work. Paper 32.3. London.

Bruce I., McKennell A. and Walker E. (1991) *Blind and Partially Sighted Adults in Britain: the RNIB Survey.* Volume 1. HMSO. London.

Campbell J. and Oliver M. (1996) *Disability Politics: understanding our past, changing our future.* Routledge. London.

Coleridge P. (1993) *Disability, Liberation and Development.* Oxfam. Oxford.

Corley G. Robinson D. and L Lockett S. (1989) *Partially Sighted Children.* National Foundation for Education Research. Windsor.

Crow L. (1996) Including All of Our Lives: renewing the social model of disability. In Morris J. (ed) *Encounters with Strangers: feminism and disability.* The Women's Press. London.

Davis K. (1993) On the Movement. In Swain J., Finkelstein V., French S. and Oliver M. (eds.) *Disabling Barriers - Enabling Environments.* Sage. London.

Davis K. (1994) Disability and Legislation. In French S. (ed.) *On Equal terms: working with disabled people.* Butterworth-Heinemann. Oxford.

Department of Health (1989) *Coordinating Services for Visually Handicapped People.* HMSO. London.

Dodds A. (1993) *Rehabilitating Blind and Visually Impaired People: a psychological Approach.* Chapman and Hall. London.

Finkelstein V. and Stuart O. (1996) Developing New Services. In Hales G. (ed.) *Beyond Disability: towards an enabling society.* Sage. London.

French S. (1989) Mind Your Language. *Nursing Times.* 85, 2, p29-31.

French S. (1996) Simulation Exercises in Disability Awareness Training: a critique. In Hales G. (ed.) *Beyond Disability: towards an enabling society.* Sage. London.

Hevey D. (1992) *The Creatures Time Forgot: photography and disability imagery.* Routledge. London.

Jackson S. and Livingstone I. (1985) *Out of the Pit.* Puffin Books. Harmondsworth.

James P. and Thomas M. (1996) Deconstructing a Disabling Environment in Social Work Education. *Social Work Education.* 18, 1, p34-45.

Lovelock R., Powell J. and Craggs S. (1995) *Shared Territory: assessing the social support needs of visually impaired people.* The Joseph Rowntree Foundation. London.

Morris J. (1991) *Pride Against Prejudice*. The Women's Press. London.

Morrison E. and Finkelstein V. (1993) Broken Arts and Cultural Repair: the role of culture in the empowerment of disabled people. In Swain J., Finkelstein V., French S. and Oliver M. (eds.) *Disabling Barriers - Enabling Environments*. Sage. London.

Oliver M. (1983) *Social Work with Disabled People*. Macmillan. London.

Oliver M. (1990) *The Politics of Disablement*. Macmillan. London.

Oliver M. (1995) Disability, Empowerment and the Inclusive Society. In Zarb G. (ed.) *Removing Disabling Barriers*. Policy Studies Institute. London.

Oliver M. (1996) *Understanding Disability: from theory to practice*. Macmillan. London.

Oliver M. and Zarb G. (1992) *Personal Assistance Schemes*. Greenwich Association of Disabled People. London.

Rieser R. (1995) The History of Disabling Imagery. In Rieser R. (ed.) *Invisible Children*. Save the Children and The Integration Alliance. London.

Schön D. (1983) *The Reflective Practitioner*. Basic Books. London.

Schön D. (1988) *Educating the Reflective Practitioner*. Jossey-Bass. San Fransisco.

Scott-Parker S. (1989) *They Aren't in the Brief: advertising people with disabilities*. King's Find Centre. London.

Shakespeare T.W. (1996) Disability, Identity, Difference. In Barnes C. and Mercer G. (eds.) *Exploring the Divide: illness and disability*. The Disability Press. Leeds.

Shakespeare T., Gillespie-Sells K. and Davies D. (eds.) (1996) *The Sexual Politics of Disability: untold desires*. Cassell. London.

Social Services Inspectorate (1988) *A Wider Vision.* HMSO. London.

[...] *agement and* [...] London.

[Stuart O.] [...] Oppression: an appropriate starting point? In [...] Finkelstein V., French S. and Oliver M. (eds.) *Disabling Barriers - Enabling Environments.* Sage. London.

Swain J., Finkelstein V., French S. and Oliver M. (eds.) (1993) *Disabling Barriers - Enabling Environments.* Sage. London.

Swain J. and Lawrence P. (1994) Learning about Disability: changing attitudes or challenging understanding. In French S. (ed.) *On Equal terms: working with disabled people.* Butterworth-Heinemann. Oxford.

Thompson N. (1993) *Anti-Discriminatory Practice.* Macmillan. London.

Union of the Physically Impaired Against Segregation (1976) *Disability Challenge.* Number 1. May.

Walker E., Tobin M. and McKennell A. (1992) *Blind and Partially Sighted Children in Britain.* Volume 2. HMSO. London.

Williams P.C. (1993) Care Management and Assessment with Blind and Partially Sighted People. In Stevens A. (ed.) *Back from the Wellhouse: discussion paper on sensory impairment and training in community care services.* Central Council for Education and Training in Social Work. London.

Zarb G. (1995) Removing Disabling Barriers: an overview. In Zarb G. (ed.) *Removing Disabling Barriers.* Policy Studies Institute. London.